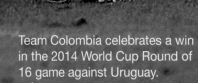

Team Colombia celebrates a win in the 2014 World Cup Round of 16 game against Uruguay.

JAMES RODRÍGUEZ

Abbeville Press Publishers
New York London

A portion of the book's proceeds are donated to the **Hugo Bustamante AYSO Playership Fund,** a national scholarship program to help ensure that no child misses the chance to play AYSO Soccer. Donations to the fund cover the cost of registration and a uniform for a child in need.

Text by Illugi Jökulsson

For the original edition
Design: Ólafur Gunnar Guðlaugsson
Layout: Ólafur Gunnar Guðlaugsson and Árni Torfason

For the English-language edition
Editor: Nicole Lanctot
Production manager: Louise Kurtz
Layout: Ada Rodriguez
Copy editor: Mike O'Connor

PHOTOGRAPHY CREDITS

Getty Images: p. 8 (Fabrizio Bensch), 15 (David Cannon), 18 (Gonzalo Arroyo Moreno), 25 (Alejandro Pagini/AFP), 26 (STR/AFTP), 28–29 (Dean Mouhtaropoulos), 30–31 (Jose Jordan/AFP), 35 (Pelé: Central Press), 35 (Maradona: David Cannon), 36 (Laurence Griffiths), 38 (Valery Hache), 40–41 (Paul Gilham), 42 (Adam Pretty), 45 (Julian Finney), 46 (Robert Cianflone), 48–49 (Michael Steele), 49 (Denis Doyle), 50 (Fabrice Cofrini/AFP), 54–55 (Clive Mason), 56 (James: Gonzalo Arroyo Moreno), 57 (Bale: Denis Doyle), 57 (Zlatan: Harry Engels), 58–59 (Denis Doyle)

Shutterstock: p. 2 (A. Ricardo), 10–11 (Jess Kraft), 10 (Action Sports Photography), 11 (Top: Danny Alvarez), 11 (Bottom: Jess Kraft), 13 (Shakira: Helga Esteb), 13 (Vergara: Featureflash), 17 (Andrey Gontarev), 18–19 (Maxisport), 20–21 (Gary C. Tononi), 28 (Martinez: Celso Pupo), 28 (Hulk: AGIF), 33 (AGIF), 34–35 (A. Ricardo), 35 (Messi: A. Ricardo), 36 (Falcao: Maxisport), 53 (Maxisport), 56 (Messi: mooinblack), 56 (Ronaldo: Natursports), 56 (Neymar: almonfoto), 63 (Jefferson Berardes)

Wikimedia Commons: p. 10 (Jose Lara), 12–13 (Luis García), 13 (Roel), 19 (Russell Watkins), 22–23 (chilangoco), 23 (Ivanics–trabajo propio), 27 (Rudolf Stricker), 43 (Olaf Kozany)

Flickr: p. 16–17 (Stephen Downes)

First published in the United States of America in 2015 by Abbeville Press, 116 West 23rd Street, New York, NY 10011.

First edition
10 9 8 7 6 5 4 3 2 1

ISBN 978-0-7892-1237-5

Library of Congress Cataloging-in-Publication Data available upon request

For bulk and premium sales and for text adoption procedures, write to Customer Service Manager, Abbeville Press, 116 West 23rd Street, New York, NY 10011, or call 1-800-ARTBOOK.

Visit Abbeville Press online at www.abbeville.com

CONTENTS

JAMES RODRÍGUEZ

Colombia's Rising Star

James Rodríguez burst onto the international scene during the 2014 World Cup, proving his significance by leading the Colombian national team to their greatest success yet in the tournament. Rodríguez scored six goals and won the Golden Boot as the tournament's top goal scorer. Experts have long expected good things from this young and daring attacking midfielder, and now Rodríguez has emerged as one of the world's most promising soccer players.

"James has grown up and matured very quickly," said Colombia's coach, José Pékerman. "Each new step that he makes surprises me, and he has great potential. He is a winner."

COLOMBIA!

James Rodriguez comes from a beautiful and remarkable country in South America.

Famous Colombians

GABRIEL GARCÍA MÁRQUEZ

(1927–2014)
Renowned author and winner of the Nobel Prize in Literature; wrote the masterpiece *One Hundred Years of Solitude.*

PABLO MONTOYA

(Born 1975)
Racecar driver who has competed and won awards in Formula 1, NASCAR, CART, and IndyCar

A view of the center of Bogotá, Colombia, with the Andes in the background

Guatapé Lake, Colombia

Colorful colonial houses on a cobblestone street in Guatapé, Antioquia, Colombia

Biggest Cities in Colombia

	City	Population
1	Bogotá	7.9 million
2	Medellín	2.5 million
3	Cali	2.3 million
4	Barranquilla	1.2 million
5	Cartagena	1.0 million

AREA 439,735 square miles
Similar to New Mexico, Texas, and Louisiana combined.

POPULATION 48 million
Similar to California and Washington State combined.

THE HISTORY

Colombians have all kinds of backgrounds.

Colombians have all kinds of backgrounds. Settlement first began in the territory now known as Colombia more than 10,000 years ago. Several indigenous tribes arrived from North America on their way to settle land and find a new home in South America.

The civilizations built by the populations in the Colombian territory were small in comparison to the mighty civilizations of the Mayans and the Aztecs to the north (Mexico) and the Incas to the south (Peru). The Colombian civilizations were crafty in many ways, however. The Quimbaya people, for example, created wonderful artifacts from gold.

Christopher Columbus sailed from Spain and arrived in Central America in 1492. Europeans proceeded to colonize the Americas, and the indigenous peoples suffered greatly as a consequence. The Europeans were often cruel, and they brought diseases with them from the Old World that killed countless natives. The area of modern Colombia was flooded with European colonizers, mostly from Spain but also from other European countries. The territory came to be known as New Granada.

After many difficulties and battles, the inhabitants declared independence in 1810. They severed ties with the Spanish and decided that their new nation would be named Colombia, after Christopher Columbus.

Colombia has experienced much turmoil, including wars with neighbors, civil wars, guerrilla warfare, crime, and inequality.

However, recent years have been more peaceful than in the past. And the nation is rich in natural beauty and versatile resources.

A street in the Candelaria district of Bogota, Colombia

A Quimbaya golden statue, approximately 1,500 years old

After Colombia separated from Spanish rule, the nation was merged with Ecuador and Venezuela. For this reason, the nations have similar flags.

Colombia

Ecuador

Venezuela

Famous Colombians

SHAKIRA

(Born 1977)
Singer and musician, model and fiancé of Gerard Pique, a defender with Barcelona in Spain

SOFÍA VERGARA

(Born 1972)
Actress known for her colorful performance in the comedy series *Modern Family*

FERNANDO BOTERO

(Born 1932)
Artist who is world famous for his paintings and sculptures of voluptuous and spherical people

SEARCHING FOR GOLD

Soccer is the most popular sport in Colombia. The country's biggest teams attract an enormous amount of spectators, and soccer stars are national celebrities. Despite the popularity of the sport, Colombia has not accumulated a high number of trophies at significant international tournaments.

The Colombian national team played its first World Cup match in 1962 in Chile. The team was unsuccessful and did not win a game in the tournament, losing to Yugoslavia and Uruguay and managing a draw with the Soviet Union. It would be twenty-eight years before Colombia took part in another World Cup—the 1990 World Cup in Italy. The team had its moments during the tournament, played to a draw with West Germany in the group stage, and advanced to the Round of 16. The Colombian team was then knocked out following a suspenseful battle with Cameroon.

The Colombian team was composed of fantastic players in the early 1990s. Players such as Andrés Escobar, the fuzzy-haired midfielder Carlos Valderrama, and the colorful goalkeeper René Higuita became celebrities in their home country when the national team gracefully clinched a place in the 1994 World Cup with a celebrated 5–0 victory over the fierce Argentinean team in Buenos Aires. Many pundits believed that victory at the 1994 World Cup was a possibility for the Colombian team. The team played a strong offensive game with an elegant style.

However, the Colombian team came up against many difficulties in the tournament. They lost to Romania and to the host United States in the group stage and failed to enter the Round of 16 as a result. Escobar, the team captain, had the misfortunate of scoring an own goal during the match against the United States. Tragically, he was murdered in revenge for the mistake when he returned to Colombia.

History mostly repeated itself at the 1998 World Cup in France. Colombia failed to advance from their group, which also included England, Romania, and Tunisia.

The 2001 Copa America tournament was held in Colombia. The hosts were victorious and celebrated the milestone for years to come. The Colombians may not have played as elegantly as before, but the team was powerful and solid. Defensive stalwart Iván Córdoba scored the winning goal in the final against Mexico.

The celebrated victory was followed by years of decline. The Colombian team repeatedly failed to enter the final tournament of the World Cup. The national team was absent from the world's greatest tournament for 16 years! However, the team eventually made it back to the World Cup in 2014, and this time led by a player named James Rodríguez.

René Higuita of Colombia shields the ball from Jürgen Klinsmann of West Germany during a 1990 World Cup match in Bologna, Italy.

THE HOMETOWN

James Rodríguez was born in the city of Cúcuta in the eastern part of Colombia. When he was still an infant, his family moved to Ibagué, a city in central Colombia.

Ibagué's population is around 650,000. The climate is especially pleasant, with temperatures averaging around 77 degrees Fahrenheit, and there is hardly any discernable difference between summer and winter.

Ibagué is located on a plateau in the Colombian Andean region. The city is surrounded by towering mountains on every side, and there are two active volcanoes close by.

Ibagué is sometimes referred to as the musical capital of Colombia—and even of South America as a whole. Massive music festivals are held in the city. Traditional Colombian music is interesting because it developed in the vast cultural melting pot that formed in the area during the colonial period as natives, African slaves, and Spaniards intermingled in work and play. One of the country's most popular musical genres is *cumbia*. It is widely respected in Colombia and elsewhere in Latin America.

Rodríguez grew up in a calm and carefree environment. He played with the youth club Academia Tolimense in Ibagué before moving to the Antioquia region in the northern part of the country to join the club team Envigado.

Revelers participate in Carnaval de Cartagena on November 11, 2011, in Cartagena, Colombia. The pageant celebrates Cartagena's independence—it was the first city in Colombia to declare independence from Spain.

Rodríguez's hometown, Ibagué, is beautiful.

JAMES BOND JR.

James Rodríguez of Real Madrid pauses before the team's Spanish Kings Cup match against UE Cornellà on October 29, 2014, in Barcelona, Spain.

FROM LEFT: James Rodríguez with Portuguese genius Cristiano Ronaldo; as a boy, Rodríguez adored Japanese soccer hero Tsubasa.

James David Rodríguez Rubio was born on July 12, 1991. He grew up in Ibagué in the Tolima region of Colombia. His father is retired soccer player Wilson James Rodríguez Bedolla. The relationship between his parents was short-lived, and his mother Maria Del Pilar Rubio later met Juan Carlos Restrepo, who became a father to young Rodríguez.

James was named after his biological father, but the family claims that both are named after none other than James Bond, the fictional British spy.

However, the name is pronounced in the Spanish way: *Ha-mace*.

As a child, Rodríguez was very fond of the Japanese anime TV series *Captain Tsubasa*. The show revolved around a boy who played soccer.

Another idol was Cristiano Ronaldo, who Rodríguez would go on to play with on Real Madrid.

When Rodríguez was growing up, soccer was everything. He was shy and had a stutter. He went to see a number of specialists, and his mother wanted him to quit playing soccer for a time so they could concentrate on the problem at hand. Rodríguez's stepfather, Juan Carlos, managed to convince the family to allow him to continue playing soccer, which was no surprise, because Juan Carlos was aware of the boy's incredible talent.

"He broke everything when he was a child," said his Rodríguez's mother. "He broke all the china and picture frames in the house and windows in his school. But he was always determined to become a professional soccer player and showed how steadfast he was in that regard when he was 13 to 14 years old."

HIS BIRTHDAY

James Rodríguez's birthday places him under the astrological sign Cancer. He does not share his exact birthday with many other world-class players, but he is in the company of other iconic Cancers in soccer, Lionel Messi and Gareth Bale.

THE YOUNG CRACK!

The word "crack" (or "*craque*") is used in many countries to refer to soccer stars the likes of Lionel Messi and Cristiano Ronaldo, the "best of the best."

Schoolchildren play soccer near the city wall surrounding Cartagena's old city.

This amusing term has followed Rodríguez for a long time, as can be seen in a news article from 2004 that details his skills during the youth tournament Pony Fútbol in Colombia. The reporters who observed the tournament were clearly impressed by the boy's talent. One gets the sense at times that the spectators are present at a world championship tournament rather than a small youth tournament in Colombia. Rodríguez receives a penalty kick after being knocked down just outside the penalty area. He readies himself and stoically gazes at the defensive wall and the goal, just like a seasoned professional. He then takes an assured shot and scores a beautiful goal directly from the corner. Everyone was witnessing the birth of a new star.

The 12-year-old Rodríguez was not shy when news reporters approached him after the final. Academia Tolimense, Rodríguez's team, came out victorious, which was no surprise given that the team boasted the tournament's top player. "I am going to be a professional soccer player," Rodríguez said, and then he dedicated the victory to his mother and stepfather.

By the age of 12, James Rodríguez had already made a name for himself—and even then he was wearing the number 10 jersey.

ENVIGADO

After showing great promise with the youth team Academia Tolimense, James Rodríguez joined the club team Envigado at the age of 14. The club is located in a city bearing the same name located roughly 200 miles from Ibagué. Envigado is twice the size of Ibagué, with a population of around 300,000, and it is situated near the metropolis Medellín. The young Rodríguez was moving ever closer to the epicenter of soccer in his home country.

Envigado was a relatively new club, established in 1989. The club was brimming with ambition and was about to reach Colombia's top league. Already, the club was internationally renowned for the quality of its youth development. The club has produced a staggering number of strong players who have gone on to join other important teams, many in Europe. Before Rodríguez, it is worth mentioning the powerful attacking midfielder Fredy Guarín, who progressed through the ranks of Envigado and later joined the Italian giants Inter Milan in 2012. Another well-known former Envigado player is Juan Quintero, who plays with the Portuguese club Porto.

Guarín and Quintero joined Rodríguez on the team that represented Colombia at the 2014 World Cup. The fact that a team as small as Envigado managed to get three players to the quarterfinal of the world's biggest soccer tournament counts as a major achievement.

Rodríguez was, of course, well provided for in the club, but he also gave his best effort, despite his young age. "He was just a kid," his mother said. "But since then he has always fought with great passion for the best positions on all the teams he has been with. Fourteen years old. It's incredible. Sometimes I can't figure it out."

Envigado advanced to the first division the same year, and during the 2007 season Rodríguez was on fire, scoring nine goals.

The fact that Rodríguez was a tremendously promising soccer player was obvious to everyone, even though he was only 16 years old. Moreover, it quickly became clear that, even though Envigado was a fruitful team for young and promising talent, it was no longer suitable for the extent of Rodríguez's skill.

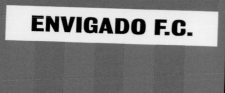

ENVIGADO F.C.

ENVIGADO FÚTBOL CLUB
Founded 1989

The Peldar Bridge in
Envigado, Colombia

BANFIELD

Following his time with Envigado, Rodríguez's path took him to Argentina. Many of Colombia's greatest soccer players have played in Argentina before heading for stardom in European soccer. The forward Radamel Falcao, for instance, played successfully with River Plate in Argentina before joining Porto in Portugal.

Banfield, a mighty soccer club who plays on the outskirts of the capital, Buenos Aires, purchased Rodríguez in 2008.

The first weeks and months with the new club proved difficult. Rodríguez was perhaps too young. He felt all alone on his 17th birthday in Argentina on July 12, 2008. He wanted to return home to the safety of his family. He worried that maybe he would never become a famous soccer player, after all.

Thankfully, Rodríguez opted against an early retirement. His spirits were lifted when another Colombian, Jairo Patiño, signed a contract with Banfield, and they became close friends.

In the following months, Rodríguez's performance during practices was so impressive that Banfield's coach, Jorge Burruchaga, invited him to join the first team. In 2009, Rodríguez became the youngest non-Argentinean player ever to play in Argentina's top division.

He immediately made it big and scored his first goal for Banfield in a match against Rosario in February 2009, setting yet another record: the youngest player ever to score a goal in Argentina's top league.

MASTER IN ARGENTINA!

Rodríguez quickly became a significant regular on Banfield's first team. And he played a large part in the team's fantastic achievements. Even though the team does not number among Argentina's strongest teams, Banfield managed to take everyone by surprise when the team won the Argentinean league in 2009.

The people of Argentina were captivated by the young Rodríguez. He was endowed with incredible shooting power and passing ability and seemed able to outrun any player.

CLUB ATLÉTICO BANFIELD

Club Atlético Banfield
Founded 1896
Biggest achievement:
Argentine league champions
(Apertura) in 2009

FAMOUS PLAYERS:

Javier Zanetti, 1993–1995; 145 games for
Argentinean national team, 1994–2011

James Rodríguez played 50 games for
Banfield from 2009 to 2010. He scored
10 goals!

THE "WHITE THREAT"

At first, Rodríguez was not a big earner with Banfield, which is not out of the ordinary, given that he was only a teenager. He took the bus to practices, and after he started playing regularly with the club's first team, his stepfather intervened. "This is what we do—I told him—I'll pay the first installment on a car, and you take care of the rest. It was a Peugeot 306, and he dubbed the car the 'White Threat.' Why the White Threat? Because the car was bright white and the engine always shut down while Rodríguez was out driving," his stepfather said." When that happened, he was forced to call me or take a cab. 'Juan Carlos, the car died.' And then I went and picked him up. We had to send him to extra driving lessons."

Jackson Martínez of Colombia makes a move in the 2014 World Cup Round of 16 game between Colombia and Uruguay at Maracana Stadium in Rio de Janeiro, Brazil.

Rodríguez's Porto teammate, known as Hulk, played for his home country, Brazil, against Cameroon at National Stadium Mané Garrincha in Brasília, Brazil.

James Rodríguez plays for Porto during the Group A UEFA Champions League match between Paris Saint-Germain and Porto at Parc des Princes on December 4, 2012, in Paris.

PORTO

Many big teams in Europe noticed Rodríguez's performance with Banfield. On July 6, 2010, a few days before his 19th birthday, Rodríguez signed a contract with the Portuguese team Porto. The price was a staggering five million euros. He remained with the club for three years and three months, during which time the team accumulated numerous titles, including three consecutive Portuguese league titles—one in each season Rodríguez was with the team—and the UEFA Europa League title.

Rodríguez breezed into the European soccer world without much difficulty following his years in Argentina. And every year, he improved by leaps and bounds. He scored a total of 32 goals in 107 games for Porto and provided numerous assists for his teammates.

PORTO TEAMMATES

Porto boasted a host of great players when Rodríguez played there, and he doubtlessly learned a lot from his comrades.

FREDDY GUARÍN

The old Envigado kid, he is a massively powerful Colombian midfielder. He later joined Inter Milan.

RADAMEL FALCAO

One of the world's greatest forwards, he is Colombia's most famous soccer player. He scored 17 goals for Porto in the 2010–2011 Europa League, which is a record. Falcao spent the 2014–2015 season with Manchester United.

HULK

The Brazilian forward and winger is renowned for great strength and speed. He later joined Zenit from St. Petersburg, Russia.

JACKSON MARTÍNEZ

Another Colombian compatriot and Rodríguez's teammate at Porto. The forward Martínez is a proficient goal scorer and an important part of the Colombian national team. He still plays with Porto.

Three of FC Porto's Colombians—from left, Radamel Falcao, Fredy Guarín, and James Rodríguez—celebrate during their successful UEFA Europa League campaign in 2010–2011.

THE THREE COLOMBIAN MUSKATEERS!

Rodríguez played 105 games for Porto from 2010 to 2013. He scored 32 goals.

FUTEBOL CLUBE DE PORTO

Futebol Clube do Porto
Founded 1893

BIGGEST ACHIEVEMENTS:

Two European Cup/UEFA
Champions League titles—
1987, 2004

THE NATIONAL TEAM

Rodríguez was part of Colombia's under-17 national team in the 2007 South American Under-17 Championship and the 2007 U-17 World Cup. He played in many tournaments with the youth national teams before the call came from the senior national team.

Rodríguez's first game with Colombia's senior team took place in La Paz, Bolivia, on October 11, 2011. The team's coach, Leonel Álvarez, entrusted the young man with the responsibility of playing in Colombia's difficult first game in the 2014 World Cup qualification round. Rodríguez was part of the starting lineup against the Bolivian team and gave a fantastic performance. His talent and control in the game were such that a seasoned player would be proud. The game was challenging and suspenseful and came to end with a 2–1 victory for Colombia. Rodríguez's Porto teammate Radamel Falcao was brought in as a substitute and scored the winning goal three minutes into injury time. Rodríguez was selected as the Man of the Match.

In the next game, Rodríguez proudly sported the sought-after number-10 jersey!

NUMBER 10!

It was a great honor for Rodríguez when Colombian national team coach Leonel Álvarez offered him the number-10 jersey. Rodríguez was only 19 at the time and a rookie on the national team. This move showed that there were high expectations for Rodríguez, and it also proved the extent of his development as a player.

The Brazilian genius Pelé established a tradition according to which daring playmakers on high-speed and agile teams wear the number-10 jersey. Pelé was unquestionably the world's leading soccer player from 1958 to 1970 and is one of the greatest players in the history of the sport. Pelé was a pure delight to watch on the Brazilian front lines, with his creativity, powerful and elegant goals, and dynamic passes.

Roughly a decade after the time when Pelé flourished, another genius entered the scene: Argentinean Diego Maradona. Maradona's brilliance as a player was no less than Pelé's, and he also wore the number 10. The number is clearly sought after by creative and daring players. More recently, another Argentinean genius, Lionel Messi, has worn the number 10, both with Barcelona and with the Argentinean national team.

Colombia's most famous number 10 was Carlos Valderrama, one of the country's legendary soccer heroes. He played midfield during the 1990 World Cup in Italy and the 1994 World Cup in the United States, as well as the 1998 World Cup in France. Valderrama was a hero in the eyes of Colombian kids when Rodríguez was growing up.

Valderrama was renowned for his precision passing and unwavering ball control. Rodríguez learned many things from observing his style of play.

Valderrama was the perfect number 10 in the eyes of Rodríguez—both a strong playmaker and leader on the pitch. "He is a big hero. I have always looked up to him and will do so for the rest of my life."

Yet Valderrama is also a big fan of young Rodríguez. "He is the new me!" Valderrama claimed after watching Rodríguez breezily outflanking his opponents on the playing field.

Pelé

Diego Maradona

Lionel Messi at the 2014 World Cup
group match between Argentina and
Bosnia and Herzegovina at Maracana
Stadium in Rio de Janeiro, Brazil

Head coach José Pékerman of Colombia consoles James Rodríguez after the Colombian team's 2–1 loss to Brazil during the 2014 World Cup quarterfinal on July 4, 2014, in Fortaleza, Brazil.

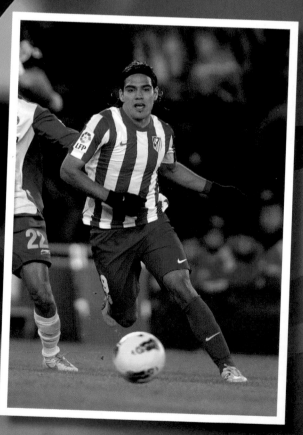

Radamel Falcao of Atlético Madrid in action during a Spanish league match against Espanyol in Barcelona on December 11, 2011

EL PROFE

Leonel Álvarez was removed as head coach of the Colombian national team in December 2011 and was replaced by veteran Argentinean coach José Pékerman, who had managed the Argentinean national team at the 2006 World Cup.

Under Pékerman, Rodríguez continued to grow and develop as a playmaker. On June 3, 2012, Rodríguez made his fourth appearance in a 2014 World Cup qualification game. He scored his first goal for Colombia, and it was an important one—the only goal in a difficult game against Peru.

Colombia confidently clinched their place at the 2014 World Cup in Brazil by landing in second place in the South American division of the World Cup qualifying tournament. Radamel Falcao was the team's top goal scorer with nine goals. Rodríguez scored three goals and was a jack-of-all-trades in the team's offensive strategy. Colombians celebrated and expected a strong performance at the World Cup.

The entire Colombian team respects their head coach, and Rodríguez is no exception. They call Pékerman "El Profe"— the Professor.

Pékerman's mother had recently passed away when Colombia played against Canada in a friendly match in October 2014. Rodríguez scored a magnificent goal and dedicated it to his beloved coach and mentor. The team huddled around El Profe and hugged him, at which the coach fell into tears.

The 2014 World Cup South America qualification

	Team	Population
1	Argentina	32
2	Colombia	30
3	Chile	28
4	Ecuador	25
5	Uruguay	25
6	Venezuela	20
7	Peru	15
8	Bolivia	12
9	Paraguay	12

Colombia played 16 games: They won 9 games, made 3 draws, and lost 4 games. The team scored 27 goals while allowing only 13.

A SUDDEN MOVE TO MONACO

ASSOCIATION SPORTIVE DE MONACO

Founded 1924
Biggest achievement:
Seven-time French league
champions, most recently
in 2000

FAMOUS PLAYERS:

Jürgen Klinsmann, 1992–
1994, 108 international
games for Germany
Rafael Márquez, 1999–2003,
125 international games
for Mexico

Monaco is a sovereign microstate, only 0.78 square miles in area with a population of 35,000. The main source of income of this constitutional monarchy is the famous casino Monte Carlo. The soccer team AS Monaco has been part of the French league since it was established.

James Rodríguez scored 10 goals for Monaco in 38 games!

In spring 2013, Monaco's owner Dmitry Rybolovlev decided to elevate the team into the group of Europe's top teams in one go. The club was just emerging from the second-highest division in France. Oodles of money were spent in order to acquire a bevy of strong players. The most famous of the bunch was the Colombian goal scorer Radamel Falcao, a former Porto player who had for the past two seasons been racking up goals for Atlético Madrid in Spain. However, Rybolovlev and the new Monaco managers were not finished. They signed a contract with the young James Rodríguez, forking close to $48 million in the deal.

a minor team was astonishing to most. The other side, however, was understandable—the Monaco officials wanted Rodríguez on their team. Rodríguez was intended to burst open opponents' defenses and create goal-scoring opportunities for Falcao and other teammates on the front line and, of course, score goals himself. And Monaco definitely benefited from the contributions of Rodríguez and Falcao. This team from the tiny nation on the Riviera played successfully in the French league, finishing in second place, which was a great achievement given that the team had just advanced from the second division.

TO THE WORLD CUP

The 2014 World Cup began on June 12, 2014. It was the 20th World Cup tournament. Brazil was host for the second time, having hosted the tournament previously in 1950. The 2014 World Cup is remembered as a particularly entertaining one. The tournament's goal tally was exceptionally high. The South American nations were especially prominent, each of them perhaps enjoying the benefits of home field.

Colombians were full of anticipation as the World Cup in Brazil drew closer. However, it was a great disappointment to learn that the goal-scoring machine Radamel Falcao would be absent from the tournament due to injuries. Falcao had scored numerous goals for Colombia over the years, and many believed that the team would struggle without him. In Falcao's absence, the Colombian team would have severe trouble scoring the necessary goals.

Yet José Pékerman and the boys had no plans of giving up. They knew that even though Falcao had been imperative to the team's success in the past, a new generation of players had arisen that were perfectly capable of holding their own. And with massive support from the populous Colombian fan base, the team got off to a great start.

The Greek team is considered defensive and tough to deal with, but the buoyant Colombian team crushed them in their first match. The Colombians were full of optimism, and their love of the game was obvious. Rodríguez was a jack-of-all-trades in the offensive game. He was a threat whenever he controlled the ball, causing fear and trembling in the Greek team. Even though expectations were high in regard to Rodríguez's performance, he leaped higher than anyone could have imagined. Rodríguez scored Colombia's third goal on a concise kick from outside the penalty area just before the end of the match. Rodríguez was chosen as Man of the Match. The small, shy kid who had struggled through his first weeks with Banfield had surely reached far—in only six years!

Konstantinos Katsouranis of Greece and James Rodríguez of Colombia battle for the ball during a 2014 World Cup Group C match.

World Cup 1st Match, Group Stage
Group C
June 14, 2014
Belo Horizonte, Brazil

Colombia vs. Greece
3–0

Pablo Armero 5'
Teófilo Gutiérrez 58'
James Rodríguez 90+3'

James Rodríguez controls the ball for Colombia as Yaya Touré of the Ivory Coast gives chase during a 2014 World Cup Group C match.

THE ROAD TO VICTORY

The Colombian team won all their matches during the World Cup group stage. The Colombian fans went crazy—it was an adventure that exceeded their wildest dreams! Rodríguez scored a goal in every group stage match, and he was at the very heart of the fantastic offensive play.

Colombia's toughest opponent in Group C was the Ivory Coast. The teams played a tight match, but the Colombians breathed a sigh of relief when Rodríguez scored on a beautiful header in the 64th minute. He then stole the ball from the Ivory Coast a few minutes later, allowing for a swift offensive attack that culminated in a goal by Juan Quintero, Rodríguez's old friend from the Envigado days. Again, Rodríguez was chosen as Man of the Match.

Given that Colombia had already clinched a position within the Round of 16, José Pékerman wanted his main star to rest for much of the team's final group match against Japan, so Rodríguez was held out of the first half of the game. Rodríguez came on as a substitute in the second half and proceeded to set up a goal, and then score a magnificent goal himself, in the final minutes of the match. He received a careful pass from the center and outmaneuvered a defender and the Japanese goalkeeper to score his third World Cup goal.

RECORD RESILIENCE

In the game against Japan, Colombia's 43-year-old backup goalkeeper Faryd Mondragón entered in the final minutes. If Rodríguez endures as long, he could participate in the 2034 World Cup!

World Cup 2nd Match, Group Stage
Group C
June 19, 2014
Brasilia, Brazil

Colombia vs. Ivory Coast
2–1

James Rodriguez 64'   Gervinho 73'
Juan Quintero 70'

World Cup 3rd Match, Group Stage
Group C
June 24, 2014
Natal, Brazil

Colombia vs. Japan
4–1

Juan Cuadrado (penalty) 17'   Shinji Okazaki 45+1'
Jackson Martínez 55', 82'
James Rodríguez 90'

A GLORIOUS GOAL!

Colombia's victory march proceeded into the Round of 16. The team faced their South American neighbors and rivals Uruguay. The latter was still recovering from the loss of a key player, Luis Suárez, who received a nine-game suspension for biting an Italian opponent during the last game of the group stage. Nevertheless, the Uruguayan team is always difficult to deal with, and the match turned into a classic. And James Rodríguez was the deciding element.

The Colombian team began on a roll, and their strategy seemed strong. Yet, nobody knew what was coming. In the 28th minute, the ball dribbled between the players as they advanced on the goal. The ball ended up at Rodríguez's feet while he was standing with his back to goal. In that position, most players would pass the ball to a teammate. Instead, Rodríguez chested the ball to the ground and then spun around and sent it thundering into the goal off the underside of the bar.

It was an incredible achievement, like a mix of gymnastics and soccer, and the crowd erupted in celebration. Television analysts replayed the goal and observed every detail, hardly believing their eyes. The goal was chosen as Goal of the Tournament and also received the FIFA Puskás Award for best goal of 2014—named in honor of the Hungarian soccer genius Ferenc Puskás.

Rodríguez scored another goal for the Colombian team in the 50th minute, with a shot fired from short range. The Uruguayans had no response and Colombia came out victorious, advancing them to the quarterfinal. Once again, Rodríguez was selected Man of the Match.

James Rodríguez shoots and scores his team's first goal during the 2014 World Cup Round of 16 match between Colombia and Uruguay.

World Cup Round of 16
June 28, 2014
Rio de Janeiro, Brazil

Colombia vs. Uruguay
2–0

James Rodriguez 28', 50'

At the end of the quarterfinal match between Brazil and Colombia, Brazilians Dani Alves and David Luiz (right) show their respect and sympathy for Rodríguez.

DEFEATED BY THE HOSTS

Colombia faced the Brazilian hosts in the 2014 World Cup quarterfinal. The match took place in Fortaleza, in northeastern Brazil. Fortaleza is a Brazilian stronghold, where the hosts are particularly difficult to beat in important tournaments, and this match proved no exception. The genius Neymar took a corner from the left in the seventh minute of the match. The ball reached Thiago Silva, who scored from close range to give Brazil a 1–0 lead. In the 69th minute, defender David Luiz scored a beautiful goal from a long-range free kick to put Brazil up by two goals. The Colombians managed to turn the tide, and Rodríguez reduced the deficit by scoring from a penalty kick with 10 minutes remaining in the match. But that was as close as it got. The Colombian team failed to equalize the game and was consequently knocked out of the tournament.

World Cup Quarterfinals
July 4, 2014
Fortaleza, Brazil

Colombia vs. Brazil
1–2

James Rodriguez '80

Thiago Silva 7'
David Luiz 69'

TOP GOAL SCORER

It is ironic that the better a player becomes in the World Cup, and the further the player's team reaches, the more his disappointment becomes at the failure to advance even further. Everyone is disappointed in the end, aside from the team that wins the ultimate award: the World Cup trophy. Brazil came out victorious in the game against Colombia, but the Brazilian team swallowed the bitter pill of defeat in their next game as they were crushed 7–1 by the German team. The Germans went on to win the world championship. Despite Rodríguez's soaring performance in the tournament, he broke down at the end of the game against Brazil and required much comforting from coach José Pékerman. However, it soon became clear to Rodríguez that there was no need to fall into a prolonged state of mourning. He played an imperative role in bringing the Colombian team the furthest it had ever reached at a World Cup, and he did so by playing an incredibly attractive attacking soccer.

Rodríguez finished as the tournament's top goal scorer with six goals, scoring at least once in each of his team's games, which is a near-unparalleled achievement in the World Cup. In fact, the last time someone had achieved something similar was when Brazilian Jairzinho scored seven goals in six games in 1970. Rodríguez was awarded the Golden Boot for his six goals.

Rodríguez was also selected to the World Cup Dream Team, and many considered that he had deserved to win the sought-after Golden Ball as the best player in the tournament. Lionel Messi eventually received the award, not without controversy.

However, while Rodríguez dried his tears, slowly realizing the extent of his performance, there was a club all the way in Madrid that had already reached a conclusion about his talents.

Top Scorers:

	Name	Country	Goals
1	James Rodríguez	Colombia	6
2	Thomas Müller	Germany	5
3	Neymar	Brazil	4
3	Lionel Messi	Argentina	4
3	Robin Van Persie	Netherlands	4

James Rodríguez with the Golden Boot

World Cup Final
Germany vs. Argentina
1–0
World Cup 3rd Place Match
The Netherlands vs. Brazil
3–0

THE DAY OF THE LOCUST

After Rodríguez scored on a penalty kick against Brazil at the 2014 World Cup quarterfinal, an enormous locust landed on his arm as if it wanted to join the celebration.

RODRÍGUEZ JOINS REAL

Rodríguez's fantastic achievements during the 2014 World Cup attracted the attention of officials from Real Madrid in Spain. Real is one of the world's most successful clubs, and they only pay for the best of the best. And even though Rodríguez had only spent one winter with Monaco, Real were ceaseless in their demands, not stopping until they had acquired the young genius. On July 22, 2014, Rodríguez signed a six-year contract with the Spanish giants for a roughly $85 million fee.

This made Rodríguez the fifth most expensive player in history, the third most expensive in Real Madrid's history, and certainly the most expensive Colombian player in history! Rodríguez had just turned 23 years old and was all smiles, telling reporters: "I've always followed Real Madrid and always dreamed of playing here. I've suffered a lot to get here and when you do that it tastes so much better. I will never forget this day. I hope to work hard, to train well, and to experience a lot of joy here. I know I am under a lot of pressure, but I am happy to face it."

REAL MADRID
Founded 1902

BIGGEST ACHIEVEMENTS:
10 European Cup/UEFA Champions League titles—1956, 1957, 1958, 1959, 1960, 1966, 1998, 2000, 2002, 2014
A record 32 Spanish league titles.

FAMOUS PLAYERS:
Alfredo di Stéfano 1963–64
Ferenc Puskás 1958–1967
Raúl 1992–2010
Zinedine Zidane 2001–2006
Ronaldo 2002–2007
Cristiano Ronaldo 2009–

AMONG THE BEST

Rodríguez made his debut with Real in the 2014 UEFA Super Cup in Cardiff, Wales, on August 12, 2014. Real Madrid defeated Seville 2–0 with goals scored by Cristiano Ronaldo. Rodríguez played 72 minutes before being substituted for by the young Spanish midfielder Isco. On August 19, 2014,

Rodríguez scored his first goal for Real against local rivals Atlético Madrid in the first leg of the Spanish Super Cup.

Rodríguez joined a team composed of pure soccer geniuses, especially on offense. Cristiano Ronaldo was a superstar, Gareth Bale had just arrived from Tottenham

Hotspur as the most expensive player in history, and the striker Karim Benzema was in unprecedented form. It was therefore no small feat for an attacking midfielder to find his way into the starting lineup. But Rodríguez was intended a bigger role, made evident by the fact that he was offered the number-10 jersey. And even though injuries slightly overshadowed the latter parts of his first season, there was no doubt that Rodríguez had proven that he was perfectly on par with the other fantastic soccer players that now played at his side.

HOW TALL IS HE?

LIONEL
MESSI
5' 7"

CRISTIANO
RONALDO
6' 1"

NEYMAR
5' 9"

JAMES
RODRIGUEZ
5' 11"

Size does not matter when it comes to soccer. The modern game's superstars range from the diminutive Lionel Messi to the giant Zlatan Ibrahimović. Rodríguez is almost right in the middle!

HEIGHT UNDER THE BAR: 8 FEET

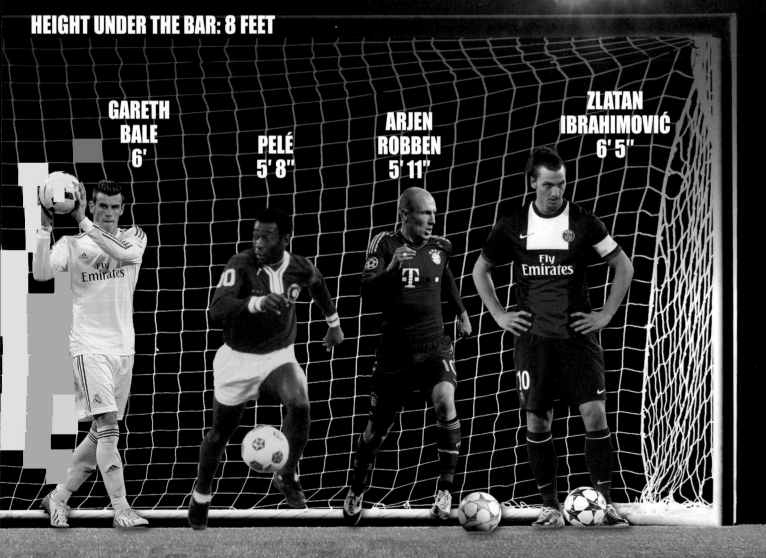

GARETH
BALE
6'

PELÉ
5' 8"

ARJEN
ROBBEN
5' 11"

ZLATAN
IBRAHIMOVIĆ
6' 5"

FAMILY MAN

Daniela Ospina was once a teenage girl in Colombia who belonged to a great family of soccer players. David Ospina, her brother, became goalkeeper for the Colombian national team at a very young age. Their mother once joked that the family was surrounded by too many soccer players.

"I do not want to see a soccer player ever in life!" she allegedly said to her 18-year-old daughter. The mother was joking, thankfully, because around that time, Daniela was introduced to a young boy who just happened to be a skillful soccer player. In fact, there was already talk of him joining her brother on the national team.

The boy was of course James Rodríguez, and it was love at first sight. They married in 2011 and their daughter, Salome, came into the world in May 2013. See a picture of little Salome with her father on the previous spread!

Rodríguez is a family man. He is said to be a practicing Christian and generally appears to be a mature and calm person. If things continue in the same vein, Rodríguez will rise to the upper echelons of the world's greatest soccer players ever—and where he goes from there is anybody's guess. The ultimate goal is, of course, raising the World Cup trophy with his Colombian teammates. Whether this dream comes true or not, Rodríguez will doubtlessly acquire countless trophies in his career to come.

Daniela Ospina is also an athlete and plays volleyball with Real Madrid. David Ospina was bought from the French team Nice by Arsenal in London following his performance for Colombia at the 2014 World Cup.

James Rodríguez Returns

The importance of James Rodríguez for Real Madrid is becoming crystal clear. On February 4, 2015, Rodríguez scored the first goal in a 2–1 win over Sevilla. Real had won 17 of their past 18 games, were at the top of the Spanish league, and seemed unbeatable with Rodríguez as creative playmaker and constant threat to the opposition. Rodríguez was, however, injured against Sevilla and was sidelined for seven games. During that period Real faltered badly, losing three games and drawing one, allowing Barcelona to overtake Real at the top of the standings.

In Rodríguez's first game back, Real returned to its winning ways in spectacular style, humiliating Granada 9–1 on April 5, with Rodríguez providing two assists. In the next game, he scored his 13th goal of the season in a comfortable 2–0 win over Rayo Vallecano, and both Rodríguez and Real were back on track.

Glossary

Striker: A forward player positioned closest to the opposing goal who has the primary role of receiving the ball from his teammates and delivering it to the goal.

Winger: A player who keeps to the margins of the field and receives the ball from midfielders or defenders and sends it forward to where the strikers await.

Offensive midfielder: A player Positioned behind the team's forwards who sees to taking the ball through the opposing team's defense, where they either pass to the strikers or attempt a shot themselves. This position is sometimes called "number 10" in reference to the Brazilian genius Pelé, who more or less created this position and wore jersey number 10.

Defensive midfielder: A player who is positioned more or less in front of his team's defense and whose central role is to break the offense of the opposing team and deliver the ball to the forwards on his own team. The contribution of these players is not always obvious, but they nevertheless play an important part in the game.

Central midfielder: The role of the central midfielder is divided between offense and defense, but mainly they seek to secure the center of the field for their team. Box-to-box midfielders are versatile players who possess such strength and vision that they constantly spring between the penalty areas.

Fullback (either left back or right back): This player defends the sides of the field, near his own goal, but also dashes up the field and overlaps with wingers in order to lob the ball into the opponent's goal. Fullbacks are sometimes called wingbacks when they are expected to play a bigger role in the offense.

Center back: This player is the primary defender for his team, and there are two or three in number depending on formation. The purpose of the center back is first and foremost to prevent the opponents from scoring and then to send the ball toward the center.

Sweeper: The purpose of the sweeper used to be to keep to the back of his defending teammates and "sweep up" the ball if they happened to lose it, but also to take the ball forward. The position has now been replaced by the defensive midfielder.

Goalkeeper: The player who prevents the opponent's goals. He is the only player who is allowed to use his hands.

Coach:

_____

CHOOSE THE TEAM

Who do you want on the field with James Rodríguez? You pick the team and you can choose whoever you want and in whatever position. You can even choose yourself and your friends if you like! And don't forget the coach!

Goalkeeper:

_____

Right back:

_____

Left back:

_____

Defender:

_____

Defender:

_____

Midfielder:

_____

Midfielder:

_____

Midfielder:

_____

Forward:

James Rodríguez

Forward:

_____

Forward:

_____

YOU SCORE A TOTALLY BRILLIANT GOAL WHEN PLAYING FOR COLOMBIA. YOU ARE MOBBED BY THE FANS AND HAVE TO WAIT ONE ROUND.

10

Use one die

YOU TAKE PART IN THE WORLD CUP, BUT COLOMBIA IS KNOCKED OUT IN THE SEMIFINALS. GO BACK 3 PLACES.

8

YOU ARE ON YOUR WAY TO AN IMPORTANT GAME BUT YOUR OLD WHITE CAR BREAKS DOWN. GO BACK TWO PLACES.

YOU ARE SURROUNDED BY LOCUSTS. WAIT ONE ROUND WHILE YOU TRY TO GET RID OF THEM.

Help James Win!

SILLY JOURNALISTS WRITE THAT YOU WILL NEVER AMOUNT TO MUCH. WAIT ONE ROUND WHILE YOU RECUPERATE.

YOU SCORE YOUR FIRST GOAL FOR YOUR NEW TEAM. GO FORWARD 4 PLACES!

5

13

YOU SCORE TWO GOALS AND PROVIDE TWO ASSISTS IN A CUP FINAL. STRIDE FORWARD 3 PLACES.

YOU PLAY YOUR FIRST GAME FOR ENVIGADO IN YOUR HOME CITY. ROLL AGAIN.

YOU SCORE A GREAT GOAL AND REAL MADRID COMES KNOCKING. ROLL AGAIN!

2

THE JAMES RODRÍGUEZ BOARD GAME!

KICK OFF